Terrific Transitions

50 Easy & Irresistible Ideas That Keep Children Interested, Engaged, and Learning as They Move From One Activity to the Next

by Ellen Booth Church

SCHOLASTIC
PROFESSIONAL BOOKS

New York • Toronto • London • Auckland • Sydney
Mexico City • New Delhi • Hong Kong

Dedication

To Jerry . . . my most wise and BEST transition in Life!

Cover design by Jaime Lucero
Cover artwork by Bari Weissman
Interior design by Sydney Wright
Interior artwork by James Graham Hale

ISBN: 0-439-20108-X
Copyright © 2001 by Ellen Booth Church
All rights reserved.
Printed in the U.S.A.

Contents

Introduction

Tran • si • tion—An act, process, or instance of changing from one state, form, activity, or place to another. (*Webster's Dictionary II*)

"The true goal of any journey is not the end destination, but the accumulation of experiences along the way."   —*Deron Levine*

Children are always making transitions, big and small, inner and outer. As they grow, they transition from infants to young children and with each transition comes more responsibility and challenge. Life is a transition from one phase to another, with many turns and obstacles along the way to make it interesting. In your classroom, transitions are opportunities for children to practice handling change.

Transitions are the journey from one activity to another and are an important part of your curriculum. Transitions can be as much a part of your lesson as anything else. And they take little time. You can introduce activities during a transition that you might not want to do in a long lesson. If successful, you can extend it at another time. You can even choose transition activities that complement a theme or unit of study.

Educational Benefits of Transitions

The following is a list of some of the skills developed during transition activities:

- ❈ increased attention span
- ❈ receptive and expressive language
- ❈ creative thinking
- ❈ problem solving
- ❈ observing
- ❈ listening
- ❈ large and small motor
- ❈ social interaction
- ❈ taking turns
- ❈ cooperation

But transitions need preparation just like any other activity. Plan for them and you'll enjoy the results. You might want to include transitions in your daily lesson plan. You may wish to choose a collection of transition activities from this book to keep on cards in your pocket. Then you can easily rotate these activities, keeping activities fresh and improving their effectiveness.

Why Transitions?

Transitions are teacher-inspired interludes actively participated in by children. Of course, children need to have free choice in activities, but that is within the clear structure of free play or center time. Without the structure of teacher-directed transitions children use their free time creatively but not necessarily constructively. Transitions are not merely a means of controlling or managing the group. They are interesting, engaging, and open-ended activities within a definite structure.

At times children need assistance in movement from a self-directed activity to teacher-directed activity (or vice versa). Children need (and want!) to know what is expected of them. By using a variety of transition activities, you can give children the direction they require while providing them with an opportunity to develop important skills.

Types of Transitions

❋ Movement Transitions—ways to transition from place to place

❋ Calming Transitions—activities for achieving serenity and the redirection of attention

❋ Action Breaks—opportunities to release extra energy through aerobics, movement, and exercise

❋ Thinking Time—thought-provoking activities that provide creative thinking and dramatic play to make the most of those extra minutes

❋ Musical Interludes—songs, poems, and fingerplays to be used whenever needed

Transition Tips

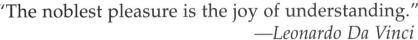

"The noblest pleasure is the joy of understanding."
—Leonardo Da Vinci

Keep these tips in mind when planning successful transitions with your children:

@ Make transitions fun and meaningful.

@ Keep a collection of fingerplays, games, and songs on index cards in your pocket for instant activities.

@ Grab students' attention with verbal and nonverbal cues. Be dramatic— use the element of surprise, facial expressions, and voice changes to indicate that something different is about to happen.

@ Indicate when a transition is about to happen, especially cleanup time. Five-minute reminders work well. You can use a stopwatch or alarm clock to mark cleanup time. Let the "object" tell that it is cleanup time. For example, saying, "The watch says it's time to clean up" may get a quicker response from children.

@ Tell children what is going to happen next. Preparing them for what is ahead helps children deal with any fear of or concern with the "unknown." In this way children understand better what is expected of them and look forward to the change.

@ Children need to be able to anticipate predictable segments of the day. Take a series of photos to show the events of the day (circle time, free play, snack, outdoors, story, etc.). Display the photos low on a bulletin board, wall, or clothesline so that children can easily refer to them during the day.

@ Take time at the beginning of the year to teach children about transitions. Show them the different signals that you will use and what you expect from the children. You may want to practice some transitions.

@ Invite children to create their own versions of the transition activities. They often have good ideas and delight in seeing others participating in the transition game of their own design.

- Clothespin markers work well for organizing cleanup. Create a clothespin for each child with his or her photo or name written on it. At the beginning of center activities, attach the clothespins to something in each center. When it is time for cleanup, children find the center in which their marker is placed and clean up that area.

- Create the role of Cleanup Inspector. The Cleanup Inspector is a hard-hat-wearing person (you!) or puppet who checks on the cleanup teams working in each area. Later in the year, when children understand expectations, they may take turns being the Cleanup Inspector.

- Have children create and decorate cleanup puppets made from gloves or mittens. These puppets love to "eat" trash and put away toys. They make cleanup time just that much more fun.

- Organize use of outdoor equipment by creating a photographic sign-up system. Let children choose a photograph or drawing of the equipment they wish to play with before they go outdoors. This will help avoid the rush to equipment.

Attention-Getting Signals

Create a signal to be used to get children's attention. Explain to children that when they hear the signal they are to freeze in place. Once they are frozen, you have their full attention to explain any directions. A few chords on the piano, a flourish on the xylophone, a distinctive drumbeat, or a bell are all good auditory signals to use. Flicking the lights can work as a visual cue as well.

Suggested attention-getting signals:

- musical instruments (bells, drums, tambourine, triangle, xylophone)

- puppet used as a classroom friend that acts as an "Announcer"

- piano chords, such as the opening to Beethoven's Fifth Symphony

- sound-effects recordings, such as vehicle noise, loud weather, or animal sounds

- whispering

- hand motions or sign language

Going From Here to There

Creative Movement Transitions

"Focus on the journey, not the destination. Joy is found not in finishing an activity but in doing it." —*Greg Anderson*

Probably the hardest transition for children to make is the movement from one activity to another. Even though the length of the journey from the meeting time rug to the door may be only a few feet, children can find many distractions along the way. Your job is to be the conductor, the inspirer, the tour guide. Keep the transition creative and happy, and children will find joy in the journey.

Creative Movement Transitions

Imagine That...

Objectives

Creative Thinking   Creative Movement
Large Motor

One way to help children move quietly and creatively from place to place is to encourage them to imagine interesting obstacles along the journey. Whether the goal is the door for recess or the tables for snack, engage children's creative minds and movements along the way.

How To

Just as you are about to excuse children to the next activity or place, put on a surprised or astonished face, gasp, and say "Something has happened to our room! Do you see it? Look! The floor is covered with eggshells. How can you walk across the floor to the door without cracking any of the shells? Okay, ready? Let's go slowly so we do not to break any eggshells!"

Variations

Change the scene and the "obstacles" frequently to keep children surprised. Try these variations, but also invite children to make up their own:

❋ We have to move through a plate of Jell-O.

❋ It must have really rained last night because now there is a river running through our classroom. How can we get across?

❋ Shhhhh, there seems to be a giant sleeping in the hallway. How can we get around him without waking him?

❋ Something happened to the ceiling. It is very low now. How can we go out without bumping our heads?

Creative Movement Transitions

Can You Do?

Objectives

Cooperation   Social Interaction
Large Motor   Problem-Solving
Creative Thinking

Children enjoy moving creatively with a partner. In this transition, children are asked to move in different ways with a partner as they go to their destination. Keep it fun and light and you will have a happy group of children lined up two-by-two and ready to go.

How To

Divide children into pairs and invite them to play a partner game as they move to the next activity.

"Let's move away from the rug in a new way today. This game is called 'Can You Do?' It is a silly way to line up. Can you and your partner make yourselves as small as possible as you move to the door? How many different ways can we move small together? Let's try it two at a time."

Variations

Try variations of "Can You Do?"

❋ Can you and your partner make yourselves as big as possible as you move to the door?

❋ Can you make yourself into a bridge for your partner to crawl under on the way to the door?

❋ Can you walk your partner like a dog to the door?

❋ Can you and your partner walk with really long legs to the door?

Creative Movement Transitions

Imaginary Shoes

Objectives

Creative Thinking   Problem Solving

Expressive Language   Large and Small Motor

What we wear on our feet can affect the way we move. Invite children to think about how they would move if they were wearing different shoes. By concentrating on moving their feet in new ways, children will focus on moving creatively instead of dashing for their destination.

How To

Introduce the imaginary shoes activity with a "magic wand" that can transform any shoes into wondrously different shoes. When you touch a child's shoes, it is his or her turn to stand up and move across the room in whatever way the shoes make them feel. For example, touch a child's shoes and say, "Allacazam Allacazear . . . your shoes be gone and giant's boots appear! How can you move from here to there with giant boots on?"

To extend and enhance the activity, play music that fits the types of shoes. Play loud, slow music and ask, "How does the music make you want to move in giant's boots?"

Variations

Try these Imaginary Shoes on for size:

❋ ice skates, snow shoes, or skis

❋ tap shoes or ballet toe shoes

❋ boots—astronaut, fishing, cowboy/cowgirl

❋ bedroom slippers

Creative Movement Transitions

Imaginary Hats

Objectives

Creative Thinking   Large Motor

Creative movement and dramatics provide opportunities for children to learn about themselves and others as they become different characters. Why not invite children to try on a new personality as they move from one place to another? The results will be an organized group of people you may not recognize!

How To

In this transition activity children move smoothly using creative thinking and impersonation. This activity works well after reading *Caps for Sale* by Esphyr Slobodkina or *Martin's Hats* by Joan W. Blos.

Don your own special hat. Then, reach into a magic sack and draw out imaginary hats one at a time as you say, "Let's see what is in sack today . . . Ah, here is a regal crown for Carlos to wear as he struts over to the snack table. And look, here is a crown for Shavonne to wear, too. Now what else is here? I see a space helmet for Mai and one for Michael. Perhaps you two can space walk together to the snack table."

You may wish to use real (or children-made) hats. Children can wear them to snack time and have a Mad Hatter Tea Party!

Creative Movement Transitions

Grab-Bag Pantomine

Objectives

Creative Thinking   Problem Solving
Large and Small Motor   Taking Turns

The world of make-believe can shift a group's mood and energy, and focus their attention in a positive way. Since children love to imitate the ways things move, use this interest to create a movement game that helps them transition from one place to another.

How To

In this transition game, one child reaches into a "grab bag" (a pillowcase or pretty bag) and takes out a picture of something that moves, such as an animal, and moves like that creature across the floor to a destination. Keep all the children involved by encouraging the ones waiting to guess the animal the child is pantomiming. Each child, in turn, chooses a card and moves like his or her animal until everyone is at the destination.

Creative Movement Transitions

Roll-Call Lineup

Objectives

Receptive Language   Listening
Cooperation

There are so many ways you can call children to line up. The trick to smooth line up roll calls is diversity. The more options you have, the more successful you will be at keeping the group organized.

How To

Play with children's names, clothing, and words during your lineup routine.

Variations

Try these fun ways to call children to leave an area to line up for the next activity:

❋ **Initial Consonant Sound Roll Call** Choose an initial consonant sound (such as *d, r, t, f*) you would like children to recognize. Call children's names replacing their original initial consonant sound with the new one. For example: For the /d/ sound you would call Tomiko, Justin, and Chelsea as Domiko, Dustin, and Delsea. Note whether children are able to recognize their names with the new initial consonant sound.

❋ **Name Cards** Write each child's name on an index card. At first, hold up the card and read the child's name aloud. You might want to include a symbol on the card so the child can learn to recognize the symbol first, then the name. As children are able, begin to hold up the cards without reading the names.

❋ **Rhyming Pairs** Distribute pairs of cards with pictures of objects that rhyme, such as *bear* and *chair*. Call one picture name of the rhyming pair, such as *dog*. The child holding that card stands up. Then call the name of the picture that rhymes with the first card, such as *hog*. This pair of children lines up. Continue until all children are in line. Over time children can guess the rhyming word card and form pairs on their own.

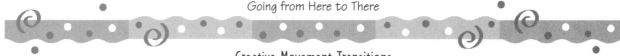

Creative Movement Transitions

If You Are Wearing...

Objectives

Receptive Language   Listening   Taking Turns

A song is a wonderful way to organize children as they are lining up. Music quickly garners children's attention. When you add children's names, clothing, or other personal attributes to the song, they listen and attend to the task at hand. It's fun to take old favorites, adapt the words, and create a new method for calling children together.

How To

Most children love the song "If You're Happy and You Know It." It is fun to sing and easy to embellish. You can focus on the colors children are wearing, their clothing, physical characteristics (long or short hair, brown eyes), or emotions (smile, frown).

Try this version of the song:
"If You Are Wearing _____, Go Line Up"
(sung to the tune of "If You're Happy and You Know It")
If you're wearing something *red*, go line up,
If you're wearing something *red*, go line up,
If you're wearing something *red*, and you can touch your head,
If you're wearing something *red*, go line up!

Variations

If you're wearing pants with pockets, go line up!
If you're wearing pants with pockets, and can do a little dance

If you have velvet brown eyes, go line up
If you have velvet brown eyes, and can look way up high

If you are wearing a big broad smile, go line up
If you are wearing a big broad smile, and can walk like a crocodile

Creative Movement Transitions

All Aboard!

Objectives

Listening   Large Motor   Taking Turns

Even in this day and age children are attracted to trains. Perhaps it is their colossal size that makes an impression on children, or a train's soulful sounds and majestic length. Whatever the appeal, just start a train movement and you will have children in line in no time!

How To

Use your favorite train song or chant but change the words to include children's names, and you will quickly have children "on track" for a transition from one place to another.

Variations

"Engine, Engine Number Nine"
(traditional chant)
Engine, engine number nine,
Running down Chicago line.
Ashley and *Joshua*, get on line,
Engine, engine number nine.

"Down by the Station"
(traditional song)
Down by the station, early in the morning,
See the little pufferbellies all in a row.
See *LaToya* and *Tran* get on the engine,
Puff-puff, toot-toot, off we go.

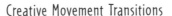

Creative Movement Transitions

The Ants Go Marching

Objectives

Listening   Large and Small Motor

A little silliness can go a long way when getting children organized. When the "sillies" are kept under control by a song and accompanying movements, children stay attentive.

How To

This popular song is a great tool for getting and keeping children lined up for a short walk around the classroom, a neighborhood walk, or field trip. Add children's names to the song to personalize it and keep them engaged.

"The Ants Go Marching"
(sung to the tune of "When Johnny Came Marching Home Again")
The ants go marching one by one,
Hoorah, hoorah!
The ants go marching one by one,
Hoorah, hoorah!
The ants go marching one by one,
Raymond stopped to beat a drum.
And they all go marching down,
to the ground, to get out, of the rain.
Boom! Boom! Boom!

Add verses and change the experience by changing the numbers of ants.

Variations

✳ The ants go marching two by two,
Juan and Kayla stop to tie their shoes.

✳ The ants go marching two by two,
Darius and Megan stop to say "Moo!"

✳ The ants go marching three by three,
Tarisha, Matthew, and Austin stop to climb a tree.

✳ The ants go marching three by three,
Gabriel, Ming, and Ian stop to look at the sea.

Creative Movement Transitions

Gooey Popcorn!

Objectives

Listening   Large Motor   Social Interaction   Cooperation

This silly movement game encourages children to work cooperatively. The recipe is a mix of one part movement, one part music, and one part dramatic play. Stir in imagination to make a "popcorn ball" of children.

How To

Invite children to pretend they are unpopped kernels of popcorn in a popper. Be dramatic. Act out "pouring" them in the popper, plugging it in, and heating them up. Children act out the following song, jumping on "Pop!" as you sing.

"I'm a Little Popcorn"
(sung to the tune of "I'm a Little Teapot")
I'm a little popcorn in a pot.
Heat me up and watch me pop.
When I get all fat and white I'm done.
Popping corn is lots of fun! Pop!

Then invite children to "pop" around the rug area for a minute. Then say, "Freeze, Popcorn! Have you ever had candied popcorn with syrup on it? Well, I am going to 'pour' gooey syrup on you so when you start popping again and when you bump into a friend you will stick together! When you are stuck to one friend, you both 'pop' your way to line up!"

Thought-Provoking Games for Waiting Time

"Too often we give children answers to remember rather than problems to solve." —*Roger Lewis*

Every teacher has experienced those awkward moments between two activities. Sometimes children have to wait for others to complete the first activity, or the whole group must wait for an activity to begin. This waiting time can be a difficult, restless time for children. What do you do with these times? Fill them with thinking play! Instead of using idle "time fillers" you can actually expand children's thinking and turn a few short moments into an active learning experience.

Thought-Provoking Games for Waiting Time

Same and Different Talk

Objectives

Increased Attention Span
Creative Thinking

Expressive Language
Social Interaction

You don't need any extra props for this game, so you can do it anywhere at any time to keep children interested and involved. Same and Different is basic to every curriculum. By making comparisons, children use the higher-order thinking skills of analysis and evaluation.

Variations

Try comparing . . .

❋ Classroom objects, such as furniture, posters, blocks, toys, library books

❋ Outdoor objects, such as trees, weeds, leaves, insects, vehicles, clouds

❋ Personal items, such as clothing, shoes, physical attributes

How To

Got a minute? Play Same and Different to get children observing and thinking in an instant. Follow these steps.

1. Invite children to observe something specific around them. For example, the trees on the playground; the classroom lights; floor tiles; their shoes or other pieces of clothing. Say, "Look at these two trees. What do you notice about the trees?"

2. Ask children to compare the trees, by asking, "How are the trees alike? How are the trees different from each other?" You may want to make a comparison to get children started. Once children begin, stand back and let the creative thinking and the discussion begin!

Thought-Provoking Games for Waiting Time

Crazy Questions

Objectives

Expressive Language   Creative Thinking
Listening

Children are accustomed to adults asking questions that have right or wrong answers. These types of convergent questions do not invite higher-order thinking or even good conversation. If you ask a child "What color is this?", there is only one right answer, and it is a one-word answer. Divergent questions invite children to think beyond surface information. They must use the higher-order thinking skills of application, analysis, synthesis, and evaluation to answer. Sounds like hard work? It's not! In fact divergent questions or "crazy" questions are as much fun as they are thought provoking!

Variations

Try these asking these "crazy" questions!

❋ What would happen if birds could talk? (change animals)

❋ What would happen if there were no television sets? Computers? Video games?

❋ Where do rainbows come from? Where does night come from? Where do clouds come from?

❋ Why do leaves change colors?

How To

There is nothing like a "crazy" question to get children's attention. When sitting with the group waiting for the snack to arrive, the movie to start, the bus or parents to arrive for pick up, stimulate a thoughtful conversation. You might say, "I wonder what would happen if Tyrannosaurus rex was alive again. What are some things you might see?" If this is too difficult for children to jump into, help them through visual imagery. You might say, "We know that Tyrannosaurus rex was really big.

Where would it sleep? Where would it live?" You might need to give one or two of your own ideas to "prime the pump" but soon you'll have a lively discussion going.

Thought-Provoking Games for Waiting Time

I Spy

Objectives

Expressive Language   Creative Thinking   Problem Solving   Observing

The trick to creating great instant thought-provoking games is to use what is around you. No special materials are required! Invite children to look for an object in the room, make up a riddle, or give descriptive clues so other children can guess. In this way, you are encouraging children to notice their environment and take a multidimensional view of their surroundings. This kind of activity stimulates important visual observation and inference skills.

How To

Keep this activity in your back pocket so that you can pull it out whenever you need to quickly get children involved and thinking. To play I Spy, say this traditional riddle (do not look at the object being described):

"I spy with my little eye . . .
something that is round and has hands and numbers. Can you find it? What is it?" (a clock)

After you have played this game several times with children, invite a volunteer to be the I Spy leader. Decorate a paper towel or toilet-paper tube with aluminum foil and shiny stickers. Let the I Spy leader look around the room using the "spy glass" to locate an object.

Variations

Describe . . .

❋ objects in the room

❋ children's clothing and your clothing

❋ each other

You may wish to graduate to objects that are not visible but children are familiar with, such as animals, vehicles, buildings.

Thought-Provoking Games for Waiting Time

How Many Ways Can You?

Objectives

Expressive Language   Creative Thinking

Thinking "outside the box" is a fun way to utilize a few minutes of time. At the same time, you are stretching children's brain power and perhaps your own! Open-ended questions stimulate creative thinking and deductive reasoning and keep children's minds engaged when you need to keep the group under control.

How To

Inspire creative thinking at any time just by asking this simple open-ended question: "How many ways can you _____?"

For example, while waiting for snack you might ask, "What are some ways you can use a banana?" Children might answer, in a fruit salad, to prop open a door, as a puppet. The answers are bound to be diverse, interesting, and possibly funny. Be prepared for children to suggest ideas you never thought of before. Remember to celebrate all children's ideas equally. There is no right or wrong answer to these questions!

Variations

Provide props for children to manipulate, or just let their imaginations run wild with these "How many ways can you _____" questions:

❀ How many ways can you use a key?

❀ How many ways can you use a plate?

❀ How many ways can you use a circle? A square? A triangle?

❀ How many ways can you use a feather?

Thought-Provoking Games for Waiting Time

Look Again

Objectives

Expressive Language   Creative Thinking

What would happen if you could change the way you look at things? It would change your experience. You can change a group's mood by inviting children to change their perception. Starting with objects and moving on to feelings helps children see that how they look at things affects their world.

How To

To play this game, you need a touch of imagination and the willingness to be flexible with your thinking. Surprise children by saying, "Quick! Look at the classroom door-way. Now view it as if it were an entrance to an imaginary world. Where does it lead? What does the world look like? Who lives there? What do they do?" The next time children walk through that door they will have a different perception of it!

Encourage children to see something they normally might find ugly as beautiful. For example, when walking with children past a big mud puddle, say, "See the mud. Now look at it as if it were a beautiful painting. What do you notice?"

> ### Variations
>
> Encourage children to look at objects or ideas as funny, scary, happy, etc.

Thought-Provoking Games for Waiting Time

You Name It!

Objectives

Expressive Language   Problem Solving   Listening

Word games are a creative way to fill waiting time and challenge children at the same time. By inviting children to think of words (or labels) for things and ideas you are asking them to use expressive language, receptive language, and problem-solving skills.

Our Favorite Colors	
Blue	Ⅲℍ
Red	|||
Green	||
Orange	
Purple	||||

How To

Start with simple games and progress to more difficult thinking activities. Suggested games:

1. **Name Your Favorite**—Choose a category such as ice cream flavors, animals, colors, movies, and songs. Ask children to name their favorites. You may wish to create an experience chart or graph to list and tally the children's choices. Help children determine which item was the most favorite.

2. **Name the Category**—In this reverse of Name Your Favorite, a volunteer names a group of objects and then the class guesses what category they belong to. For example, the child names *fish, cats, dogs, hamsters,* which all belong to the category pets.

3. **Name That Thing**—Give clues that are characteristics of an object or animal. Start with simple general clues, such as *It is big.* Progress to more specific clues, such as *It carries children to school.* Count how many clues were needed for children to accurately guess the thing.

Thought-Provoking Games for Waiting Time

Starter Pictures

Objectives

Creative Thinking   Small Motor   Taking Turns   Cooperation

Adults often draw or doodle when they are waiting. Why not do a class doodle together? Starter pictures are just like they sound—a start to a drawing. You never know what will come out of it!

How To

If possible, begin this activity with a reading of the story, *Harold and the Purple Crayon* by Crockett Johnson. On a sheet of butcher paper draw an unusual shape or a wiggly line. Ask children what the shape reminds them of. Let children turn the page in different directions to get different ideas. Then let children come up one at a time and add to the drawing. When they are finished, encourage children to give the artwork a title. Don't worry if it doesn't look like "something" at the end. It just might be a work of modern art!

Variations

❋ Use different media for your starter pictures. Try using paint. Cut pictures from magazines to make a collage. Or even make starter sculptures of clay or Play-Doh.

❋ Display works by modern artists for children to study (available in art books and on the Internet). Painters such as Paul Klee, Joan Miro, Jackson Pollock, Pablo Picasso, and Henri Matisse all worked in styles similar to the group picture you may have created. Be sure to share the titles of the works children enjoy.

Thought-Provoking Games for Waiting Time

Puppet Interviews

Objectives

Increased Attention Span
Listening

Expressive Language
Social Interaction

Creative Thinking

A puppet is an effective tool for redirecting children's attention. Keep a collection of puppets hidden away near your meeting area or a waiting area. Earmark these as special puppets you use for Puppet Interviews, not the ones children use during playtime. If they are kept special in this way, the interest level will remain high.

How To

Have you ever noticed how children are sometimes speechless when they have puppets on their hands? They may only able to communicate nonverbally with the puppet. Puppet Interviews keep children interested and involved with puppets in a positive way. In the process, children also learn how to converse with puppets.

Before showing the puppet, say, "I have a friend I would like you to meet, but she is kind of shy. Do you think you can help her feel comfortable? Maybe if you ask her some questions about herself she will feel more at ease!" Let children ask the puppet anything—even silly questions. They might ask about where the puppet lives, whom she lives with, what she likes to do or eat, or about what makes her happy.

Thought-Provoking Games for Waiting Time

The Magic Story Bag

Objectives

Expressive Language   Creative Thinking
Listening   Taking Turns

Spontaneous storytelling can be a fun way to inspire thinking. It is especially good for those times when you need something quick to do. Some children can tell stories without props or direction, but most young children benefit from the use of visual or tactile clues to get the story started, and keep it going.

Variations

❄ Tape record the story as children tell it and place it with the materials in your listening center.

❄ Set up different themes for the stories by using different containers and contents. For example, a suitcase can be a travel story; a shopping bag can be a shopping trip; a toolbox can be a fix-it story.

How To

Place a collection of toys and dolls in a pretty pillowcase or bag. Show the bag and say, "I have a magic story bag filled with parts of a story. The only problem is that I forgot the story! Can you help me? Perhaps if you reach in the bag and take out one of the characters we can create the story together?" You can begin by taking out the first object and starting the story with a "Once upon a time" opening. For example, you might pull out an umbrella and begin, "Amelia was bored. She wanted something fun to do. She looked outside and saw that it was raining. It was a rainy Sunday, but Amelia wanted to play soccer." Then let a volunteer reach into the bag and take out an object and continue the story. The story might continue something like this:

(toy telephone) Amelia called her friend Jackson and said that she wanted to play soccer. "But it's raining, Amelia," Jackson said. "We can't play outside!"

(Ping-Pong ball) Then Amelia had an idea! She invited Jackson over to play inside her house. Jackson came over and they played soccer using their fingers as players and the Ping-Pong ball as a soccer ball!

Thought-Provoking Games for Waiting Time

What's in the Bag?

Objectives

Creative Thinking   Problem Solving
Small Motor   Taking Turns

Guessing games are about the simplest thought-provoking tool you have in your transitions toolbox. They require children to use deductive reasoning and creative thinking skills. Bound to entertain and involve, these games are a winner every time because children love the element of surprise!

Variations

※ Play the game in reverse. Invite children to find something in the room to hide in the bag while you close your eyes. Children give clues while you guess what's in the bag.

※ Ask children to bring something from home to put in the surprise bag. Give them a category, such as "something that makes a sound," "something that is soft," or "something that is very little." Be sure children bring their objects in brown paper bags so no one peeks ahead of time. Then play the game having each child give clues for his or her special object.

How To

Use a shopping bag or pillowcase to create a beautifully decorated surprise bag. Place a familiar classroom object, such as a stapler, in the bag and give simple clues about it. Invite children to feel the object through the bag. Ask, "Can you guess what's in the bag?" As children get more adept at guessing, progress to more difficult objects and clues.

Calming and Centering

Activities to Regain a Sense of Peace

"A wild person with a calm mind can create anything"
　　　　　　　　　　—Eric Maisel

Sometimes things get just a bit too loud or hectic during the day. Happily, children can often shift quickly to a calmer mood if they are given a simple activity that redirects their attention. Instead of growing frustrated, try some of these simple activities that calm and refocus.

Activities to Regain a Sense of Peace

Pass the Quiet Stone

Objectives

Increasing Attention Span   Calming   Taking Turns   Centering

Refocusing children's attention is often all that is needed to change a mood. One way to shift their attention is to invite children to move from an active outer focus to a quieter inner focus. All it takes is an interesting prop, movement, or idea.

How To

Pass the Quiet Stone is a simple centering activity that helps children stop spinning out and instead spin inward.

Call the children together in a seated circle. Place a beautiful stone, crystal, or rock in the center of the circle. It should be large enough so children cannot put it in their mouths or be tempted to throw it. Invite children to look at the rock for a few moments. (It is good to change the object frequently so children stay interested in observing it.) Then you might say, "I am going to pick up the stone, and feel it as I hold it for a few moments. When I am finished, I will pass it to the person next to me to hold. We will silently pass the stone around the circle until it returns to me."

Variations

Pass these items around the silent circle:

❋ a nature item, such as a pretty flower, piece of wood, or leaf

❋ a vegetable or fruit that is later washed and tasted by the group

❋ something delicate, like a paper or cloth doily, or a downy feather

Activities to Regain a Sense of Peace

The Spin Inside Me

Objectives

Self Awareness   Large Motor   Focusing Attention

Exaggeration is a wonderful way to eliminate or change a mood or action. When children deliberately experience a behavior they are doing unconsciously, they can actually exhaust and change it!

How To

Is the classroom's energy spinning? By inviting children to deliberately spin around and around and then stop, you can calm the group. Use a signal to get children to stop what they are doing and freeze. Then say, "Let's take a spin break. Stand up and put your arms out to your sides just like you are a half-opened umbrella. Make sure you cannot touch anyone. Take one slow spin around to make sure that you will not bump into anyone. When I count to three, everyone spin around and around until I tell you to stop. When I say stop, lie down on the floor right where you are. Ready? One, two, three, spin!" Don't let children spin too long or they will get dizzy.

When children are lying on the floor instruct them to take a deep breath and feel the "spin inside" that continues even after they stop moving. Tell them to go back to their previous activity when the inside spinning stops.

Activities to Regain a Sense of Peace

Shout It Out!

Objectives

Creative Thinking
Focusing Attention

Listening
Verbal Expression

Is the noise level rising? Take it a few steps higher and you can actually lower it. Often children make noise because they need to. Trying to quiet them without acknowledging this is often a temporary fix. By deliberately having children make sounds in different ways in a controlled setting you can meet and satiate their need to shout.

How To

You may wish to use a visual cue, such as blinking the lights or shutting the lights off and shining a flashlight around the room to get the children's attention. Once you have their attention, ask them to freeze in place and listen. You might say, "Did you notice that we are getting too loud? Now, watch me. I will be the conductor of the Shouting Orchestra. When I give the signal, start shouting. As I move my hands up, get louder. When my hands show cut or stop, everyone needs to stop shouting. Keep your eyes on me." (It is a good idea for children to practice starting and stopping with the conductor before trying this activity.) Repeat this activity a few times to get those shouts out!

You might want to invite children to try making other kinds of sounds as well. For example, let children make a silly sound like a bleep or a blurp.

Do a Follow the Leader game by making a silly sound and having children echo it back to you. By the time you're done, they will be laughing and quieted down.

Activities to Regain a Sense of Peace

The Teeny, Tiny Sound Game

Objectives

Creative Thinking   Listening   Focusing Attention

By inviting children to play with sound in a game, you can help them focus and center their energy and find a peaceful way to spend the rest of the day in your classroom.

How To

Ask children, "Find a comfortable place to stand while I take you on a sound trip. There is a teeny, tiny sound hiding in your big toe. Can you find it? Hear it? Okay, make the teeny, tiny sound. Very quietly now. Any way it wants to sound. Now it is starting to move up your body. Now it is in your knees. It is getting a tiny bit louder. It moves to your belly. It is getting louder. It is in your chest and louder still. It is in your throat and just about to jump out of your mouth. It is loud now. Shout it out of your mouth!" Usually by this time children are both energized, relaxed, and ready to go back to regular classroom activities.

Activities to Regain a Sense of Peace

The Quiet Listening Game

Objectives

Increased Attention Span   Listening   Peace

The flip side of making noise is listening for it. And, of course, the only way to hear sounds is to be quiet. The world is filled with sounds that children may not be aware of. When children focus their attention on sounds in their environment they begin to hear these ambient sounds. At the same time, they become more aware of the sounds they are making.

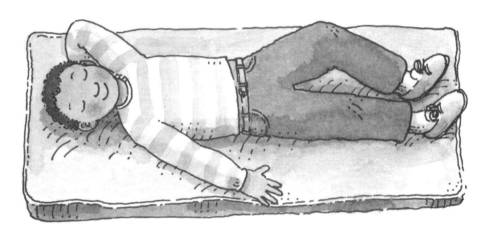

How To

Inside or out, this listening game helps children become aware of the existence of sound and the power of quiet. Invite children to sit or lie down comfortably in a space, not touching another child, where they can hear your voice. You might say, "We are going to be very still and quiet so we can hear all the sounds around us. Let your body relax into the floor (ground) so that you feel like a puddle. It might help if you close your eyes and open your ears. Without telling me, think about the sounds you are hearing. What are they? Where do they come from? Feel the sounds. Feel the quiet between the sounds. Now listen and feel the sounds inside you. Feel the quiet inside you, too. Rest. Breathe the quiet inside you." Pause for about a minute (longer with more practice). "Slowly open your eyes and look around the room. Welcome back!"

Activities to Regain a Sense of Peace

Heartbeat–Drumbeat

Objectives

Increased Attention Span   Listening   Relaxation   Centering

The warming and dependable sound of a heartbeat can be very calming. A steady beat is a place we all can go back to in times of stress. It has been found that many times when people gather together their hearts adjust to beat together in the same slow rhythm. The same thing can happen when we replicate a heartbeat with a drum. We can soothe agitation and pounding heartbeats into the slow pulse of peace.

How To

In Native American cultures, the drum is called the "heartbeat of Mother Earth." It is worth it to buy a good-quality hand or floor drum for your classroom (Remo is one manufacturer). The sound of a good resonant drum is transcendent and can shift the mood of a class. It can also be used to prepare children for quiet time or nap.

Gather children for a calming and centering break by using your hand or a padded stick to beat the rhythm of a slow, quiet, and steady heartbeat on a drum. The heartbeat is played to the rhythm of four:

drumbeat 1–2; pause 3–4; drumbeat 1–2; pause 3–4.

Repeat this steady, soft rhythm as long as needed.

Children will hear and feel the beat and soon come to join you in the circle. You might say, "Can you feel the beat inside you? Listen to your heart and feel it beat with the drum."

You may wish to invite one or two children to join you in keeping the beat.

Activities to Regain a Sense of Peace

Tense and Release

Objectives

Increased Attention Span   Large and Small Motor   Sensory Motor   Relaxation

Children may not even be aware that they are carrying tension in their bodies, although they usually express it with excited behavior and movements. We all can be tense at times, but relaxing is often difficult. By deliberately experiencing and exaggerating the tension, we can get to the other side—relaxation!

How To

One way to get children to be aware of the tension in their body is to have them purposely tense their muscles one at a time and then release them. This is a major principle of many exercise and yoga routines.

Invite children to find a comfortable place to lie on the floor. Make sure they are not touching each other. Say, "We are going to feel the muscles in our bodies. Listen carefully to the directions. First, start with your toes. Scrunch up your toes as tight as you can. And hold. Let them go. Now your legs. Tighten your muscles. Squeeze and hold. Let them go." Continue moving up the body. End by asking them to tighten their entire body and release. Then, be silent for a few moments to encourage children to feel the calm they have created in their bodies.

Activities to Regain a Sense of Peace

Be a Marionette!

Objectives

Creative Thinking   Large and Small Motor   Social Interaction   Cooperation

Have you ever watched children move when they are relaxed? They are so loose that even if they fall they usually don't get hurt. They just roll and move with the direction of the fall. That is the gift of relaxed movement—a sense of ease and safety.

How To

An extension of the Tense and Release exercise is one in which children use the image of a loose and relaxed object to empower their movements. Brainstorm different objects that are relaxed and loose in their movements. Children might suggest stuffed toys, dolls, and puppets. In this activity, you simply play quiet movement music and invite children to move as if they were a stuffed doll or puppet.

One useful image is of a marionette. Some children may not be familiar with a marionette so it is helpful to bring one to school for demonstration purposes. Ask children to find a partner. Then say, "Choose one person to be the puppet (marionette) and the other to be the puppeteer. The puppeteer can stand on a low chair in back of the puppet and pretend to move it with strings." Play slow music for the marionettes to move to. You may wish to give specific directions to guide children in calm, slow movements.

Activities to Regain a Sense of Peace

Hear a Story—Feel a Story

Objectives

Increased Attention Span　　Creative Thinking　　Listening　　Relaxation

Have you ever felt the calm created by the sound of a quiet voice? There is something about the measured tones of a calm, clear speaking voice that relaxes and soothes. Combine this technique with beautiful words, and the effect is transporting.

How To

How can you make story time a different experience? Invite children to sit or lie with their eyes closed. Children will use their imaginations to create the visual parts of the story or poem as you read. Students will be more relaxed than when they are trying to see the pictures in the book.

Suggested books:

Little Fox Goes to the End of the World by Ann Tompert (Scholastic)

When the Sun Rose by Barbara Helen Berger (Philomel)

Grandfather Twilight by Barbara Helen Berger (Philomel)

The Nightgown of the Sullen Moon by Nancy Willard (Harcourt)

Festival in My Heart: Poems by Japanese Children edited by Bruno Navasky (Harry Abrams)

You might want to read a good chapter book over several days and weeks. Choose ones that have short and engaging chapters such as *Half Magic* by Edward Eager (Harcourt). In addition, play story recordings for children. Audio versions of favorite books work well because they are familiar to children and quickly engage their minds.

Activities to Regain a Sense of Peace

Don't Just Do Something...

Objectives

Increased Attention Span   Listening   Visual Perception   Self Reflection

In today's culture, children's lives are getting more and more scheduled. There is less time for quiet reflection. Taking a moment to *not do* is an essential part of creating peace both inside and out.

How To

When we give the mind some quiet task to focus on, it can calm and center the entire being. Through quiet perception games, children can learn to calm their minds and bodies quickly and easily. Invite children to sit comfortably in the meeting area of your room. After children are comfortable, you might say, "Without saying a word, I want you to look around the room and notice something that interests you. Sit still. Look at it carefully and notice everything you can about it without touching it." Pause. "Now, pretend you can touch it. Without saying a word, think about how it would feel if you could touch it." Pause. "Now, find something different to look at." Pause. "Pretend you can touch it. Without speaking, think about how it feels." Pause. Find something else on which to focus.

Activities for Creating Songs Together

"After silence, that which comes nearest to expressing the inexpressible is music." —*Aldous Huxley*

Music has a wonderful way of calming, or at least redirecting, us all. It can be used to gather children into a group, to get their attention, to make peace, and solve problems. Think of music and sound activities as the best (and perhaps, the fastest) medicine in your emergency first aid kit.

A musical interlude should be short, fun, expressive, and participatory.

Activities for Creating Songs Together

The Bear Went out the Window

Objectives

Receptive Language   Creative Thinking
Listening

Have the children got a case of the sillies? Use them in a song to get children under control and have a good laugh together. Just take a familiar song and change the lyric to something totally ridiculous. Then invite children to add their own silly verses to it. Not only will children refocus their attention but they will use creative language skills at the same time!

Variations

Try these other silly lyrics to familiar songs!

❄ She'll Be Comin' Round the Playground (sung to the tune of "She'll Be Comin' Round the Mountain")

❄ Five Little Bananas Jumping in a Tree (sung to the tune of "Five Little Monkeys")

❄ If You're Silly and You Know It, Make a Face! (sung to the tune of "If You're Happy and You Know It, Clap Your Hands!")

How To

Using the melody of the children's song, "The Bear Went over the Mountain," change it to the silly song, "The Bear Went out the Window." You might want to keep a bear puppet available to act it out. Usually by the second line children will be singing along with you. Then pass the puppet and encourage children to suggest other silly things the bear can do, and put them in the song. Urge children to use objects around them in the song. For example, the bear went under the rocker, the bear went over the easel. This is engaging and good practice with prepositional phrases.

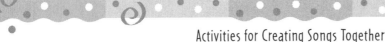

Activities for Creating Songs Together

Hand and Finger Rhymes

Objectives

Receptive Language   Listening   Small Motor

Get children's attention in a creative way with hand and finger rhymes. By focusing children's attention on the motions to a song, you can easily capture their wandering attention.

How To

Try some of these rhymes.

"This Little Monster" (said to the rhythm and motions of "This Little Piggy")
This little monster went to day care,
This little monster climbed trees,
This little monster ate green beans,
This little monster had fun!
And this little monster went
Thump, thump, thump, straight through the woods!

"Jump, Cricket, Jump"
The cricket is sleeping curled up in its nest. (show a fist)
Snap goes a branch and disturbs his rest. (snap fingers)
Up jumps the cricket from his sleep. (show hand opening and jumping)
And rolls back down without a peep. (show hand rolling back to sleep position)

"Five Fat Elephants" (said to the motions and rhythm of "Five little Monkeys")
One fat elephant standing on a string,
One step, two step, such a funny thing.
He thought to himself, "What an amazing feat!"
Then he called another elephant to bring his feet.

Two fat elephants standing on a string . . . (continues up to five)
Five fat elephants standing on a string. Boom! Too many things!

Activities for Creating Songs Together

Sounding

Objectives

Listening   Cooperation   Vocal Expression   Auditory Perception

When is sound music, and when is it noise? What may sound like music to one person may sound like fingernails on a chalkboard to another. Playing with sounds and tones can be used to fill extra time, calm a group, and to get children's attention. Just start singing a tone, any tone, and the children will look at you right way.

How To

You don't need any props for this transition activity, just your voice. The creation of different tones, one at a time, that are then blended together can spontaneously create music with children. This technique is called "sounding" and is used by professional musicians as well as classroom teachers. It is simple to do and you do not have to be a musician or singer to do it.

Just say "Ah" and hold the tone as long as you can. Then say to children, "Can you make this sound, too?" After children have mimicked your tone, invite them to make different tones or sounds while you are holding yours by saying, "Now, try to make and hold a different tone while I am holding my tone. Listen to my sound, and make a sound that feels good with it." What often starts out sounding like cacophony naturally ends up as harmony. Children will learn to listen and blend with each other.

Activities for Creating Songs Together

Sounds That Can't Be Spelled

Objectives

Listening   Auditory Perception
Verbalization

Using the philosophy "If you can't beat 'em, join 'em," you can get children's attention by amplifying their sounds. If what a noisy group sounds like is a bunch of unconnected sounds and syllables, try saying *"Blawhipjrtft."* Children will notice you immediately and will be amused at how strange the teacher sounds today!

Variations

✳ Let volunteers take turns being the Sound Leader.

✳ Make hand and foot sounds or rhythms for children to replicate.

How To

To begin this call-and-response game, you might say, "We are going to play a quick sound game. I am going to make a silly sound that can't be spelled easily. Then you make it back to me. Ready? *Woohuupp!*" Children repeat the sound and then you change to a different one. Be creative. Try different types of sounds such as, long and low, high and squeaky, clicky, creaky, and even scary. Be prepared for lots of giggles along the way. End with soft sounds to calm the group.

Activities for Creating Songs Together

Sonic Unwinding

Objectives

Listening   Self Awareness   Calming

Has your classroom ever been too noisy? Why does it happen? Children's physical and emotional energy level can increase as the day progresses expressing itself with sound (noise). By giving children a specific time and method to express this energy, they learn to unwind in an entertaining way.

How To

Children's noise level can be enough to make you want to put your fingers in your ears. In this activity that is just what children are going to do while they are making sounds. Since everyone has their fingers in their ears the sound doesn't bother anybody!

Sonic Unwinding allows children to express built-up tension by releasing sounds. To introduce the activity, you might say, "Did you notice how loud we are getting today. It makes me want to put my fingers in my ears. So let's all do just that. When I say 'Go!' I want you to put your fingers in your ears and make any sound you want. Try starting soft and change your sound to be loud and soft. Watch me the whole time. When I take my fingers out of my ears and motion 'cut,' stop and take your fingers out of your ears. Ready? Go!"

Activities for Creating Songs Together

Pass a Rhythm

Objectives

Listening   Non-Verbal Communication

Rhythm is an important part of the musical experience for children and a potent transition tool. Just start a rhythm with your hands and before long children will be joining in. And, if they are creating a rhythm with you, then you have their undivided attention.

How To

All you need is your most important musical instrument—your hands! Don't say anything, just start tapping or clapping a rhythm. Start with simple rhythms and add more complicated rhythms as you go along.

Try tapping on different parts of your body, on the floor, or on the furniture. You might want to start with a simple Follow the Leader–style rhythm, in which children copy and join in creating whatever rhythm you are making. You can then Pass the Rhythm, on to a volunteer who leads with his or her own rhythm. Let children "pass the rhythm" around the group, making sure everyone gets a chance to lead a rhythm, until it comes back to you. Then make a slower and quieter rhythm to end the activity on a peaceful note.

Variations

* Play a rhythmic question-and-answer game. Beat a rhythm "question" and have children "answer" by beating a rhythmic response. This can be done as a call and response with you or with pairs of children communicating back and forth.

* Add drums or claves (rhythm sticks) to give the rhythm games a new dimension.

Activities for Creating Songs Together

Miss Minny Monkey

Objectives

Listening   Small Motor

Children love songs that involve hand movements and change. These keep children interested and involved as they try to remember the next motion. Use them when trying to get children focused.

How To

Similar to the song "Bingo," this song eliminates a word with each verse and replaces it with a motion. Children must listen and watch carefully to be able to do the song correctly. This is a good attention keeper during a transition time. By the last verse there are few words to sing, but there are a lot of giggles!

"Miss Minny Monkey" (sung to the tune of "The Battle Hymn of the Republic")
Miss Minny Monkey had a bee upon her nose.
Miss Minny Monkey had a bee upon her nose.
Miss Minny Monkey had a bee upon her nose.
And she bopped it right in the head . . . OUCH!
Create motions for the words "Monkey," "bee," "nose," "bopped," and "OUCH." Then with each verse drop one word and do the motion instead.

Activities for Creating Songs Together

My Fingers Are Starting to Wiggle

Objectives

Receptive Language   Body Awareness
Large and Small Motor

Has your class got the wiggles? This musical interlude invites children to wiggle more and more. By the end of the song children should have their wiggles wiggled out and be ready for the planned activity.

How To

Children begin by making wiggling motions with their fingers. In the next verse they add a new wiggling body part, and another with each subsequent verse, until by the end their entire body is wiggling!

"My Fingers Are Starting to Wiggle"
(sung to tune of "The Bear went over the Mountain")
My fingers are starting to wiggle, (wiggle fingers)
My fingers are starting to wiggle, (wiggle fingers)
My fingers are starting to wiggle, (wiggle fingers)
Around and around and around! (wiggle hands in a circle)

With each subsequent verse add a new body part, such as hands, arms, feet, legs, head, even tongues. End with "My body is starting to wiggle" and children wiggle their whole bodies.

Activities for Creating Songs Together

Sing It to Me!

Objectives

Creative Thinking   Listening
Self Expression

When is a song not a song? When it is a discussion! Musical improvisation is a great way to engage children's creative minds and hearts. You don't need any words or props to do it, just a willingness to play with sound and melody. This is a great activity to do when there is just a little extra time to use creatively.

How To

Instead of *talking* to children, sing to them. What would happen if you sang a question to children instead of talking to them? Can they sing an answer in response? Yes, they can!

This activity is a variation on call-and-response songs. The difference is that there are no set lyrics or tune. You might say, "I am going to sing a question to you while you listen. When I am done you sing your answer back to me. I will listen and then respond to you. We can go back and forth with our questions and answers to make a conversation. Ready? Set. Listen!" Then sing a question to a simple melody. Don't worry if it sounds "in tune" or pretty. For example, sing "What color is your shirt?" to the tune of "Good Morning to You." Then the child might sing, "My shirt is blue." Remind children that in any conversation it is important to listen to each other before responding.

Variations

❈ After children have had a group musical conversation with you, invite them to do it with a partner. Ask them to think about what they want to ask or discuss and then sing it!

❈ Transition out of this activity by singing instructions for where to go next.

Activities for Using Extra Energy

"This time, like all times, is a very good one—if we but know what to do with it"
—Ralph Waldo Emerson

Young children need to move. A lot! Unfortunately, children often do not get enough opportunity to move during their day at school and at home. Active movement is often relegated to recess time once a day. The results can leave children with energy that needs to be expressed in fun, constructive ways. Unexpected Action Breaks sprinkled throughout your day help children let off the steam that is building inside them.

Create a signal to let children know that it is time for an Action Break. It can be a song, a motion, a sign, or a sound. You may wish to have children help you choose the signal. When children notice the signal they will know to stop and listen for directions to a fun Action Break.

Activities for Using Extra Energy

Musical Friends

Objectives

Listening   Large Motor
Cooperation

Children need to express emotions and feel a sense of connectedness. Short, active, and fun games that build cooperation are ideal Action Breaks.

How To

This "connection" game can be played anytime, anyplace. Use a signal to get children's attention. Tell children that they are going to play a quick Musical Chairs-type game. You might say, "I am going to play music for you to move to. You are to move freely and safely to the music around the room. But listen carefully because when the music stops, find a friend to hug. Then when the music starts again you move to the music again. Be ready to find a friend to hug when the music stops." This activity allows children an opportunity to move in constructive ways and feel a mutual connection.

Activities for Using Extra Energy

Two-Minute Aerobics

Objectives

Listening   Large Motor   Body Awareness

A shift in the classroom mood can be as simple as raising children's heart rates. When children are breathing deeply and their blood is pumping, you will see a visible change in their emotions, attitude, and physical well-being. No props are needed—just a leader giving simple directions for children to follow.

How To

Hectic day? Take an aerobic break. You don't need a large space. In fact, this activity works well if children stop what they are doing in the classroom and just do the exercises from where they are!

You might begin with a stretching activity. "Let's get comfortable in our space by placing our feet shoulder-width apart and slightly bending our knees. Now reach up high with one arm and slowly bring it down. Now reach up high with the other hand and slowly bring it down. Can you touch the floor with one hand? Now the other? How about both hands flat on the floor?"

Add any other stretches to this warm-up. Then invite children to balance on one foot, then the other. Move up to hopping on both feet, and then alternate feet. Have children run in place, twirl around, or do jumping jacks.

End the Action Break with a cool-down. You might invite children to pretend they are ice cubes melting in the sun, or a car that ran out of gas, or a sleepy bear preparing to hibernate.

Always start slow and gain momentum in the movements. Then end with slow movements and stretching for a peaceful transition back to classroom activities.

Variations

❊ Sing and move to "Head, Shoulders, Knees, and Toes."

❊ Take a "wiggle break" directing children to wiggle individual body parts adding one at a time until they are wiggling all over. End by taking the wiggles away one at a time.

Activities for Using Extra Energy

No-Fail Simon Says

Objectives

Listening   Large Motor   Following Directions

Young children love to play group games but can feel disappointed when the object of the game is to get someone "out." Change your favorite competitive group games to cooperative ones by finding ways to keep children "in" the game! These games work well as short Action Breaks and are more fun for everyone. At the same time, they teach sharing and caring.

How To

Playing Simon Says with a special leader hat each time lets children know that it is time to play as soon as you don the Simon hat. To begin, you might say, "We are going to play Simon Says, but in a new way. When I say 'Simon Says do this,' you do it. But if I *don't* say 'Simon Says,' you *do not* do it. But this time don't worry if you make a mistake. If you do, we'll just giggle and go back to playing the game. Nobody is out!"

Invite children to take turns wearing the hat and being the leader.

Variations

❊ Play the game with two groups and two leaders. If one person misses in one game she/he just moves to the other game. Don't forget to have two Simon hats!

❊ Play a Simon Says Follow the Leader game. Let children form a line behind you. Walk making an interesting movement, and say "Simon Says wiggle your arms." Children follow and imitate the movement. Then let children take turns leading the line. Finally, take back the lead and begin making smaller and slower movements as you bring children quietly back to their activities.

Activities for Using Extra Energy

Classroom Orchestra

Objectives

Creative Thinking

Auditory Perception

Problem Solving

Taking Turns

Action Breaks are positive outlets for extra energy. In fact, an Action Break helps prevent problems on rainy days, when a trip to the playground is unlikely.

How To

You may wish to cue this game with a few chords on a piano, a guitar, or a classroom xylophone. A dowel, smooth stick, or a ruler will work as a conductor's baton. To initiate the game you might say, "We are going to make a Classroom Orchestra. Quick, look around you for an object that makes a sound. When you have your instrument, make its sound until you see me motion 'cut' with my baton." Give children time to look for an object and make the sounds before moving on to the next step.

Then you might say, "Now I want to hear the instrument you found. When I point to you, play your instrument." After each child has had a chance to solo, lead them as a full orchestra. Some good songs to use are "If You're Happy and You Know It, Make a Sound" or "When the Kids (Saints) Go Marching In."

Variations

✽ Specialize! Instruct children to look for paper objects that can make a sound. Also try wood objects, metal, cloth, big, or small objects to use as instruments in the orchestra.

✽ During activity time have children create instruments with recycled materials, such as oatmeal boxes, paper-towel tubes, or plastic soft-drink bottles. Keep the instruments in a basket to use when playing Classroom Orchestra.

Activities for Using Extra Energy

Weight Lifting!

Objectives

Large Motor   Strengthening   Body Awareness

When large muscles are not used enough they can tighten and become difficult to control. The result can be children who move erratically and bump into things, and each other. By providing an activity that targets specific muscles, you are providing an outlet for extra energy and strengthening children's muscles at the same time.

How To

In this activity children look around for something they can easily and safely hold in their hands. Items might include unit blocks, picture books, small toy trucks, and even dolls. To begin you might say, "Let's work our muscles for a few minutes. We are going to be weight lifters! Everyone look around you for something you can hold as a weight. Got it? Hold the weight in your right hand with your arm straight down at your side. Now, bend it up and down at the elbow. Up and down, up and down. Let's count to ten. Now switch to the other hand." Demonstrate how to move each time you change the exercise. Be creative and often change their positions, the weights, and the movements. Let children suggest other weight-lifting moves.

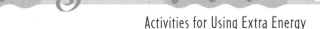

Activities for Using Extra Energy

Mirror Movements

Objectives

Creative Thinking   Large and Small Motor   Social Interaction   Cooperation

By moving together in a simple partner game during an Action Break, children can experience a sense of connection with a friend and release some energy, too!

How To

The next time you need an active but peaceful break, play this simple Mirror game. After you have the children's attention, you might say, "Have you ever watched yourself move in the mirror? What happens? What does the reflection do? Find a partner. One of you will be the mover and the other will be the reflection in the mirror. I will play some music for you to move to. Do simple movements for your 'mirror' to imitate. When the music stops, freeze. Then trade places and move to the new music." Play a variety of music, inviting children to adjust their movements to the different tempos and sounds.

Variations

❋ To make Mirror Tags, cover paper disks or plastic lids with aluminum foil, punch a hole in the top, and tie string or yarn through the hole. One child in each pair wears the Mirror Tag to indicate which child in the pair is the mirror. These help children remember who is the mirror and who is the mover.

Activities for Using Extra Energy

Peanut-Butter-and-Jelly Break

Objectives

Receptive Language   Listening
Large and Small Motor

A good laugh can turn the tide of a stressful day. Story songs are effective Action Breaks. These active, playful, and often humorous activities invite children to participate with their minds, bodies, and imaginations.

How To

A story song can be played anywhere, anytime. There is no need to gather children together, they can stop whatever they are doing and join this Action Break wherever they are. All motions are done in cheerleading style. Have children stand to do this one.

"Peanut Butter and Jelly"
Peanut butter, peanut butter (*reach arms high to the right*)
and jelly (*reach arms down and to the left*).
Peanut butter, peanut butter (*reach arms high to the right*)
and jelly (*reach arms down and to the left*).

First you get the peanuts and you pick 'em, you pick 'em,
you pick 'em, pick 'em, pick 'em (*pretend to pick peanuts*).
And you smash 'em, you smash 'em, you smash 'em,
smash 'em, smash 'em (*pretend to smash between your hands*).
And you spread 'em, you spread 'em,
you spread 'em, spread 'em, spread 'em (*pretend to spread on bread*).

Next you get the berries and you pick 'em, you pick 'em
you pick 'em, pick 'em, pick 'em *(pretend to pick berries)*.
And you smash 'em, you smash 'em, you smash 'em,
smash 'em, smash 'em *(pretend to smash between your hands)*.
And you spread 'em, you spread 'em,
you spread 'em, spread 'em, spread 'em *(pretend to spread on bread)*.

Then you take the sandwich and you bite it, you bite it,
you bite it, bite it, bite it *(pretend to bite sandwich)*.
And you chew it, you chew it, you chew it,
chew it, chew it *(pretend to chew sandwich)*.
And you swallow it, you swallow it, you swallow it,
swallow it, swallow it *(pretend to swallow but have difficulty because it is so sticky)*.
MMMmmmm MMMMmmmm! *(try singing peanut butter and jelly again but with mouth stuck together!)*

Be prepared for peals of laughter at the end!

Activities for Using Extra Energy

Take a Hike!

Objectives

Creative Thinking   Listening   Large Motor   Imagination

Variations

Try these other places to "hike"!

❅ the beach

❅ outer space

❅ the desert

Groups of children and adults together in close proximity can produce physical and emotional tension. Children bump into each other and things. It is our responsibility to create enough space to promote classroom harmony.

How To

Taking a classroom "hike" is an effective way to relieve tension. An imaginary walk can turn your space into a mountain range. In so doing you will transport children from the tight confines of your four walls to another place and time. And as they walk, they will be burning some of that extra energy, too.

To begin the hike, you might say, "Everyone meet me at the rug for a 'hike.' Let's pretend that the walls of the classroom are gone and now we are surrounded by high mountains. I see a path over there that will lead us up the mountain. It is narrow so we will have to hold hands in a long line." As children join hands, guide them around the room and even out into the hall pointing out beautiful views, dangerous passes, and strenuous climbs. End the walk by bringing them back to the rug and reality!

Activities for Using Extra Energy

An Ant's-Eye View

Objectives

Expressive Language
Large Motor

Creative Thinking
Perception

Children have a gift for pretending. With just a simple suggestion, they can become almost anything. A short pretend break may be all you need to create a sense of calm in your classroom. And taking on another persona is a good way to expand and shift our perceptions of the world.

Variations

❋ Explore the room as a cat, a fish, a lion, an elephant, a walrus, and other animals children are familiar with.

❋ Be a part of nature, such as a tree, the wind, a waterfall, a rock.

How To

Invite children to take a break to pretend to view the world as animals see it. You might say, "I wonder what the world looks like to an ant. Let's get down on the floor and become tiny ants crawling around the room. What do you see? How does the world look? How do you feel?" Find a destination in your room (such as the circle-time area) to gather children and discuss their experience. Ask questions about how it felt and what they saw when they were ants.

Activities for Using Extra Energy

Jump Rope Without the Rope!

Objectives

Creative Thinking   Large Motor

Perhaps you have not been able to take children outdoors because it has been raining for days. Or perhaps the indoor gym has been unavailable all week. Whatever the reason, children need to give voice and movement to this wonderful kinetic energy.

How To

Ready! Set! Jump! Try some jump-rope chants indoors without the ropes. Stop the action in the classroom with one of your favorite freeze signals, and say, "Let's pretend we each have a jump rope. Can you see it right there in front of you on the floor? Yes, there it is. Pick it up and jump with it. Be sure to stay in one spot. Try a few warm-up jumps and then we will say some fun jump-rope chants as you jump." Give children a chance to jump freely first and then start the chants.

"Dinosaur Dinosaur"
(sung to the tune of "Teddy Bear, Teddy Bear")
Dinosaur, dinosaur, turn around.
Dinosaur, dinosaur, touch the ground.
Dinosaur, dinosaur, jump up high.
Dinosaur, dinosaur, touch the sky.
Dinosaur, dinosaur, reach down low.
Dinosaur, dinosaur, touch your toe.

Variations

❈ Replace "dinosaur" with other animals or children's names. How would a robot, a field mouse, or an astronaut jump?

Notes

"The secret of genious is to carry the spirit of childhood into maturity."   —*Thomas Huxley*